SELF-ESTEEM PASSPORT™

Created by Michael Krawetz

An Owl Book
Henry Holt and Company · New York

*This book is dedicated to my late brother Jerome Krawetz,
who taught the living how to live.*

Special thanks to his friends
Dave LaBelle and Brian J. Fitzpatrick
for their invaluable help.

Copyright © 1980, 1984 by Michael Krawetz
All rights reserved, including the right to
reproduce this book or portions thereof in
any form.
Published by Henry Holt and Company, Inc.,
115 West 18th Street, New York, New York 10011.
Published in Canada by Fitzhenry & Whiteside,
195 Allstate Parkway, Markham, Ontario L3R 4T8.

ISBN 0-8050-0218-9

Henry Holt books are available at special discounts
for bulk purchases for sales promotions, premiums,
fund raising, or educational use. Special editions
or book excerpts can also be created to specifications.

For details contact:

Special Sales Director
Henry Holt and Company, Inc.
115 West 18th Street
New York, New York 10011

First published by 21st Century Growth
Passports Company in 1980.
First Owl Book edition—1984

Printed in the United States of America
7 9 10 8 6

Neither this book nor its publisher is associated in any way
with the United States Government or any of its agencies.

SELF-ESTEEM PASSPORT
CONTENTS

How the Passport Works 4
Bearer's Name and Address 5
Identification Page 6
Be Proud of Your Looks Visa 7
Physical Attributes Visa 8
Self-Confidence Visa 10
Acceptance of Faults Visa 12
Sense of Humor Visa 13
Personal Courage Visa 14
Choosing to Risk Visa 16
Playing to Win Visa 18
Power of Failure Visa 20
Giving Up Resentments Visa 22
Being Your Own Best Friend Visa 24
Respect for Others Visa 25
Forever Young Visa 26
Your Uniqueness Visa 27
Freedom from Guilt Visa 28
Capsulize and Internalize Visa 29
Validation 32

4

HOW YOUR SELF-ESTEEM PASSPORT WORKS

This is your United States of America Self-Esteem Passport. It validates your allegiance to yourself. It will help protect you against feelings of inferiority and inadequacy.

With your newly discovered self-esteem strengths—found inside the pages of this document and written in your own hand—you will have the power to transform the quality of your life. You will direct your mind to set your success pattern.

Possession of this Self-Esteem Passport will allow you to move forward naturally—growing in self-worth and self-love—because this document provides you with an *immediate* awareness of your combined strengths, triumphs, and personal achievements—the essential self-esteem catalysts.

This document permits you to progress without delay or hindrance to your life's goals and destinations. If you travel during times of stress and trouble, carry it with you. Its contents will provide you with the strength and comfort of your own self-acceptance.

Your Self-Esteem Passport is valid for life. It can be modified by entering—and then internalizing—your new self-esteem achievements in the summary section of this document.

> *"Sow a thought, and you reap an act;*
> *Sow an act, and you reap a habit;*
> *Sow a habit, and you reap a character;*
> *Sow a character, and you reap a destiny."*
>
> —Samuel Smile

5

SELF-ESTEEM PASSPORT

Date of Issuance

BEARER'S NAME AND ADDRESS

_____

_____

_____

Telephone: _____

NOTICE TO PASSPORT HOLDERS

This United States of America Self-Esteem Passport™—issued to all persons regardless of age, race, or creed—will permit the bearer to experience a new sense of self after honestly completing all visa entry sections.

However, you will be in violation of the rules governing your Self-Esteem Passport if you persist with the following negative attitudes which undermine your newly gained self-esteem: An unwillingness to let go of living in the past, habitual self-condemnation and feelings of worthlessness, and professing allegiance to self-pity, pessimism, resentment, and dishonesty.

"So much is a man worth as he esteems himself."

—Rabelais

IMPORTANT: This United States of America Self-Esteem Passport is NOT VALID until completed and signed BY THE BEARER.

NAME		SEX	
BIRTH DATE	BIRTHPLACE		
HEIGHT	HAIR COLOR	COLOR OF EYES	
SINGLE OR MARRIED	FAVORITE OCCUPATION		
NAMES AND AGES OF CHILDREN	FAVORITE HOBBY		
	FAVORITE SPORT		
	_____ SIGNATURE OF BEARER		

7

BE PROUD OF YOUR LOOKS
VISA SECTION

Paste in a favorite photograph of yourself on this page. In the space below, list the reasons why you selected it. Concentrate on physical self-acceptance. Determine, for yourself, what is attractive about you. Admiring all of your features bolsters your self-esteem because it is the highest form of self-acceptance.

> Paste Photo
>
> in this
>
> space

_____
_____
_____
_____
_____
_____
_____
_____

8

PHYSICAL ATTRIBUTES
VISA SECTION

A realistic self-image will bolster your self-esteem. Accepting your body—whether overweight, underweight, or out-of-shape—reinforces your self-worth because acceptance stops self-hate and self-condemnation. Once you've acquired acceptance, you can then gently change any part of yourself—without self-putdowns—and further strengthen your self-worth.

In this section, list the many physical parts of yourself which you proudly accept. Include your dimensions, physique, sexy points, strengths, stamina, and contours. If you're modest, ask a friend to help you complete this section.

(Example: I have heavy but shapely thighs, a friendly smile, and a prominent nose that gives me a lot of character.)

_____

_____

_____

_____

_____

_____

_____

> *"It is no easy thing for a principle to become a man's own unless each day he maintain it and work it out in his life."*
>
> —Epictetus

9

PHYSICAL ATTRIBUTES
VISA SECTION

– PART 2 –

"Beauty in things exists in the mind which contemplates them."
—David Hume

10

SELF-CONFIDENCE
VISA SECTION

You do many things well that you've always taken for granted. Your job, running your home, hobbies, cooking, repairing broken appliances, excelling in school and at athletics, etc. Endorsing yourself for your achievements reinforces your self-worth. In this section, fill in your personal accomplishments.

(Example: I've worked up to a four-mile run every day—and I never miss an outing. I'm able to sew most of my own clothes and save hundreds of dollars every year.)

_____
_____
_____
_____
_____
_____
_____
_____
_____

> "Because a thing seems difficult for you, do not think it is impossible for anyone to accomplish. But whatever is possible for another, believe that you, too, are capable of it."
>
> —Marcus Aurelius

11

SELF-CONFIDENCE
VISA SECTION

– PART 2 –

"No one can make you feel inferior without your consent."

—Eleanor Roosevelt

12

ACCEPTANCE OF FAULTS
VISA SECTION

It's human to have faults but inhumane to condemn yourself for having them. Some faults you can change. Others will remain. Accept your faults and bolster your self-esteem. In this section, list your faults and how they may be offset by your virtues.

(*Example: I may be stubborn, but I am persistent and dependable.*)

_____
_____
_____
_____
_____
_____
_____
_____
_____
_____
_____
_____

"A man must have his faults."

—Gaius Petronius

SENSE-OF-HUMOR VISA SECTION

Humor is a vital part of life. It offsets solemn or troubled times. It keeps us from taking ourselves too seriously. If we can laugh at our past disappointments—and use the laughter to help provide new insights—we have given ourselves self-compassion, the cornerstone of all self-esteem. In this section, list some of the past hardships you've endured, but can now put into perspective with a touch of laughter.

(Example: I'm better off without my repossessed car. Now the finance company is stuck with a lemon that leaks in the rain, conks out in direct sunlight, and occasionally chases dogs.)

_____

_____

_____

_____

_____

_____

_____

_____

_____

"A merry heart doeth good like a medicine but a broken spirit drieth the bones."

—Proverbs

14

PERSONAL COURAGE
VISA SECTION

Everyone has moments of personal courage in life but those important events are often forgotten in the passage of time, or because modesty and memories of previous setbacks get in the way. Remembering your personal courage milestones—whether they were helping a poor swimmer to safety or giving your first speech in front of a large audience—fortifies your self-esteem. Recalling those times of bravery will remind you that you are self-reliant and capable of heroic action. You know you can tackle tough situations because you've done it before.

In this section, list incidents of personal courage you have experienced, from childhood to the present.

(Example: In grade school, I defended a classmate who was being treated unfairly by a bully. Years later, I drove through a dangerous snowstorm to deliver medicine to a sick friend.)

_____

_____

_____

_____

_____

_____

_____

> *"There is a proper dignity and proportion to be observed in the performance of every act of life."*
>
> —Marcus Aurelius

PERSONAL COURAGE
VISA SECTION

– PART 2 –

"The surrender of life is nothing to sinking down into acknowledgement of inferiority."

—John C. Calhoun

16

CHOOSING TO RISK
VISA SECTION

Choosing to risk strengthens your self-image. It shows that you have confidence in your judgement and are willing to overcome fear, boredom, or complacency in order to bring about change. Deliberately taking a chance implies that your decision to pursue a certain course is rational—whether it's getting married or divorced, moving to a new community or career—and that you're prepared to deal with either failure or success. If you succeed, you will enjoy a new vitality and sense of accomplishment. If you don't, the experience will strengthen your resolve to risk again because you've tested your courage and know you're able to go on. In this section, show how you have benefited from risks you have taken.

(*Example: I was always afraid to travel alone but, after the divorce, I fulfilled a lifetime dream and visited Alaska by myself. I have become my own person.*)

_____

_____

_____

_____

_____

_____

_____

_____

"Great deeds are usually wrought at great risks."
—Herodotus

17

CHOOSING TO RISK
VISA SECTION

– PART 2 –

"It is only by risking our persons from one hour to another that we live at all."

—William James

18

PLAYING TO WIN
VISA SECTION

Playing to win can often make the difference between failure and success. It means going after a goal with persistence and the unwavering resolve to succeed. If your attempts to become a winner have resulted in repeated setbacks, it's time to examine your strategies. Are your objectives reasonable? Could you be standing in your own way without even knowing it? Get in touch with your inner self. Are you unconsciously choosing to fail—or remain an underachiever—because you fear that positive changes will require living up to greater expectations? You can become a winner, which is far more rewarding than going through life as a loser, if you deal with your self-defeating patterns.

In this section, list examples of how you "snatched defeat from the jaws of victory," and indicate how you can avoid similar results in the future.

(Example: I never spoke up during employee brain-storming because I felt that no one would be interested in what I have to say, but my holding back may have kept me from being recognized by my boss. Now I realize that being able to present my ideas well is part of winning on the job, if I want to be promoted.)

"In the long run men hit only what they aim at."
—Henry David Thoreau

19

PLAYING TO WIN
VISA SECTION

– PART 2 –

"You don't learn to hold your own in the world by standing on guard, but by attacking and getting well hammered yourself."

—George Bernard Shaw

20

POWER OF FAILURE
VISA SECTION

Failure is a teacher and can be the source of much personal growth. Experiencing failure—and learning to judge your own capabilities—demonstrates that you have the strength to accept life's challenges. Never condemn yourself for not succeeding. That's being unfair to yourself. See failure for what it really is: an opportunity to discover that future success lies in another strategy or direction. You will achieve your next goal if you learn from your past mistakes. In this section, show how some of your past failures could lead to new achievements.

(Example: I tried many times without success to break the cigarette habit on my own, but I finally realized I couldn't do it alone and signed up for a stop-smoking workshop. I haven't smoked for six months and I can now taste food.)

_____
_____
_____
_____
_____
_____
_____
_____
_____

"Life is either a daring adventure or nothing."
—Helen Keller

21

POWER OF FAILURE
VISA SECTION

– PART 2 –

"A minute's success pays for the failure of years."
—Robert Browning

22

GIVING UP RESENTMENTS
VISA SECTION

Relinquish your resentments—they're only unhappy memories of past experiences that once crossed your life. It doesn't matter who was to blame. Letting go of your disappointments releases you from the mental imprisonment of reliving yesterday's troubles. You're also rid of the all-consuming need to exact revenge. Your self-esteem is automatically increased because you no longer view yourself as a tragic unfortunate who was wronged—and forever a victim of that unpleasant situation. By being forgiving—both to yourself and others responsible for the hurtful incident—you automatically eliminate your mind's existing inventory of trouble-provoking grudges and bad memories. Freeing yourself from resentments creates a brand-new blueprint for present-day happiness and a chance to go for the gold! In this section, describe how resentments have trapped you in the past and why that won't happen again.

(*Example: I resented being poor and having to work my way through school, and my constant bitterness only made me feel worse about myself. If I finally let go of hating the past, I can be free to enjoy my present success in life.*)

_____
_____
_____
_____

"Let us forget and forgive injuries."

—Don Quixote

23

GIVING UP RESENTMENTS
VISA SECTION

– PART 2 –

*"Better by far you should forget and smile
than that you should remember and be sad."*

—Christina Georgina Rossetti

BEING YOUR OWN BEST FRIEND
VISA SECTION

You have a friend for life—yourself! Friendships provide comfort and strength and must be nourished with gentle deeds and loving actions. In fact, being your own best friend and having a strong self-esteem are synonymous. In this section, list the steps you have taken to become your own best friend.

(Example: I signed up for the French class today. I wanted to take the course for the last three years. Then as a reward I made plans for a two-week vacation.)

_____
_____
_____
_____
_____
_____
_____
_____
_____
_____

> "No one can harm the man who does himself no wrong."
>
> —St. John Chrysostom

RESPECT FOR OTHERS
VISA SECTION

A vital self-esteem builder is to admire, respect, and appreciate the uniqueness of other people. No two people are alike. Recognizing the differences in others will provide you with your own special place of importance in this world and strengthen your own self-esteem. In this section, list some of the original qualities of other people and why you admire them.

(*Example: My mother is a remarkable cook. My best friend is a truly witty conversationalist.*)

_____
_____
_____
_____
_____
_____
_____
_____
_____
_____

"We can help one another find out the meaning of life.... But in the last analysis, each is responsible for 'finding himself.'"

—Thomas Merton

26

FOREVER YOUNG
VISA SECTION

Thoughts, attitudes, and actions—and not the actual passage of time—determine old age. Resistance to growth and new ideas saps the life force. Rigid thinking blocks self-renewal. Hope and anticipation are two factors which help keep you eternally young. In this section, list the actions you have taken to remain forever young.

(Example: I study dance twice a week in a studio full of students fifteen years my junior.)

_____
_____
_____
_____
_____
_____
_____
_____
_____
_____

> "We do not count a man's years until he has nothing else to count."
>
> —Ralph Waldo Emerson

YOUR UNIQUENESS
VISA SECTION

You're an original. There's no other person in the world like you. In this section, list the traits that make you a unique person. That's why you're irreplaceable.

(Example: I don't have a selfish bone in my body. I really can make people laugh and enjoy themselves.)

_____
_____
_____
_____
_____
_____
_____
_____
_____
_____
_____
_____

"Remember that the value of a man is not measured by what he has, but by what he is."

—Pope John Paul II

28

FREEDOM FROM GUILT
VISA SECTION

There's really no need to punish yourself for past mistakes by feeling guilty. Guilt cripples your self-esteem by trapping you in the memory of past failures. It creates low self-worth. There is life without guilt. It means learning from your past mistakes—and not condemning yourself for them.

In this section, list the guilt-producing experiences which once made you feel bad about yourself, but which you now choose to eliminate from your growing self-esteem inventory.

(Example: I once felt badly that I moved away from my parents' hometown. But now I've made a new life for myself and they're proud of me.)

_____

_____

_____

_____

_____

_____

_____

_____

"The greatest minds are capable of the greatest vices as well as the greatest virtues."

—René Descartes

CAPSULIZE YOUR NEWLY DISCOVERED SELF-ESTEEM STRENGTHS IN THIS SECTION AND INTERNALIZE THEM

After you've honestly answered all of the preceding Self-Esteem Passport visa entry sections, you now have living proof—authored in your own hand—that you're a very special and accomplished person.

In this section, capsulize all of your newly discovered strengths. Was there a self-esteem attribute not covered in this passport? Enter it on these next pages.

Your self-esteem discovery process doesn't end with the completion of this document. From here, your new self-esteem traits must be consciously affirmed in your own mind—just like learning the alphabet as a youngster—to ensure their continuance.

Memorize, repeat, and internalize your self-esteem attributes until they become part of your consciousness. At that point, your new self-esteem will become as automatic as breathing.

_____

_____

_____

_____

_____

_____

*"I am larger, better than I thought.
I did not know that I held so much goodness."*

—Walt Whitman

30

CAPSULIZE YOUR NEWLY DISCOVERED SELF-ESTEEM STRENGTHS IN THIS SECTION AND INTERNALIZE THEM

– PART 2 –

_____
_____
_____
_____
_____
_____
_____
_____
_____
_____
_____
_____
_____
_____
_____
_____

"As a man thinketh, so is he, and as a man chooseth, so is he and so is nature."

—Ralph Waldo Emerson

CAPSULIZE YOUR NEWLY DISCOVERED SELF-ESTEEM STRENGTHS IN THIS SECTION AND INTERNALIZE THEM

– PART 3 –

_____

_____

_____

_____

_____

_____

_____

_____

_____

_____

_____

_____

_____

_____

"The next thing most like living one's life over again seems to be a recollection of that life, and to make that recollection as durable as possible by putting it down in writing."

—Benjamin Franklin

VALIDATION OF YOUR SELF-ESTEEM PASSPORT PROTECTS YOU AGAINST LOW SELF-WORTH

Congratulations! You have just validated your United States of America Self-Esteem Passport. Your own words and self-assessments—written in the previous visa entry sections—affirm your worthiness and self-esteem.

Do not lose this document. It will now help guide you through life, protecting you against self-doubt, self-deprecation, a low self-esteem, and fear of success.

To fully ensure the success of this passport's effectiveness, carry it and remember its special contents at all times. Refer to them repeatedly because you are the source of your own strengths and achievements. Dwell on your strengths. Resist self-condemning thoughts. Respect yourself and others will too.

You are the bearer of a Self-Esteem Passport and are entitled to the pursuit of happiness and the accompanying high self-worth. This is your life and your new self-esteem. Begin living it now.

—Michael Krawetz
SELF-ESTEEM PASSPORT EDITOR

"The Universe is change; our life is what our thoughts make it."

—Marcus Aurelius